WHAT I WANT MY KIDS TO KNOW

A Father Leaves a Legacy of Advice, Wisdom and Faith

Charles Teddy Bourn

WHAT I WANT MY KIDS TO KNOW

Published by Dowe Publishing
P.O. Box 110
Nordegg, Alberta, T0M 2H0, Canada
info@dowepublishing.com

ISBN 978-0-9880031-0-1

Printed in Canada

For Cynthia, the best wife I could have hoped
for and a wonderful mother to our children.

CONTENTS

THE BACKSTORY

For various reasons, all three of our kids graduated from high school at the same time. No, they weren't triplets! In the months before this milestone in their lives I began thinking about how I might be able to help them as they left home for college, jobs and the real world. I'm sure that many parents feel the same way. As a lay minister, I was looking for a topic to preach about in our small, local church, so, I put my thoughts down on paper and delivered them over a couple different Sundays under the title, "What I'd Like My Kids to Know."

I had preached in church before, but this was the first time that a couple people asked me for my notes. I was flattered and told them that I would be happy to share them after I put them in a more presentable form. That was a few years ago now, and I'm finally getting around to making them more presentable!

I'm thankful for Elena and David's request to share my ideas. This encouragement inspired me to think that perhaps others would be interested as well. I hope that it is useful to you or someone you love.

P.S. — By the way, our three kids all just got married . . .   in the last four months!

A SUCCESSFUL LIFE

Make these six steps a habit and you will be successful. That doesn't mean that you will never have problems, but you will be blessed. I call it SWEEPS.

S. Sleep - It's fundamental to everything you do. Get enough of it.

W. The Word - Read and meditate on God's Word, the Bible. It is a remarkable book full of the secrets of success and meaning, for this life and the one to come.

E. Eat Right - Without the right fuel the fire fizzles.

E. Exercise - Take care of your body, and it will take care of you.

P. Pray - The earnest prayers of a righteous person do much good.

S. Serve - Help others and give of yourself and your resources. They will be glad you did, and you will be glad you did.

Life is about choices and commitment— choose wisely and then commit fully. Joshua was a good example of this when he said, "... choose today whom you will serve.... But as for me and my family, we will serve the LORD." Joshua 24:15

Nothing worthwhile comes easy. "Good planning and hard work lead to prosperity, but hasty shortcuts lead to poverty." Proverbs 21:5

Honor God by believing in yourself and trusting yourself. Satan tells non-Christians to, "Believe in yourself — only." He tells Christians, "Don't believe in yourself — or anyone else."

Always be honest. It's like truth or consequences. Tell the truth *or* there will be consequences (bad). It is also, tell the truth *and* there will be consequences (good).

Appreciate simple, everyday things.

Keep busy, but not so busy that schedules or things come before people or God.

Always remember... you are loved, just the way you are now.

When something breaks or stops working, including relationships, there is a two word question that can help you fix it... "What changed?" If you can identify the problem you are well on your way to solving it.

I first thought of this when trying to fix computers at work. Often the path to repairing the computer was through finding out what the user was doing just before things went wrong. Usually it was due to things like loading new software, opening an email attachment that contained a virus or moving the CPU to a new location.

So, for example, if you and your friend or spouse are at odds with each other ask, "What changed?" Then you can get to the root of the problem.

Life Is A Battle

Expect attack. "Stay alert! Watch out for your great enemy, the devil. He prowls around like a roaring lion, looking for someone to devour." 1 Peter 5:8

Be encouraged and be an encourager. "As soon as I pray, you answer me; you encourage me by giving me strength." Psalm 138:3

Satan was having a garage sale one day and had all his well-used tools of attack and temptation on sale... greed, envy, lust, pride, etc. One of his demons noticed a particular tool with a very high price tag. "Why is this tool so much more expensive than all the others?", he asked. "Oh," said Satan, "that is my Silver Wedge of Discouragement. It's my most valuable tool because with it I can pry my way into the lives of our enemies, the Christians, and then I can use all my other tools on them!"

Be defensive. Put on your armor. "Put on all of God's armor so that you will be able to stand firm against all strategies of the devil." Ephesians 6:11

Be offensive. Pick up the sword. "Put on salvation as your helmet, and take the sword of the Spirit, which is the word of God." Ephesians 6:17

Pray. "Pray in the Spirit at all times and on every occasion. Stay alert and be persistent in your prayers for all believers everywhere." Ephesians 6:18

Don't kid people about their unchangeable features.

Don't think about or discuss important or difficult things when you're tired or hungry. This is especially important in marriage.

Don't be surprised when heartache happens. "I have told you all this so that you may have peace in me. Here on earth you will have many trials and sorrows. But take heart, because I have overcome the world." John 16:33

It will get better.

Don't be too proud or afraid to let others help you.

Forgiveness

A grudge is a heavy thing to carry.

Work at restoring broken relationships.

Ask for forgiveness and forgive.

Forgiveness is like taking an antacid.

The first to apologize is the bravest. The first to forgive is the strongest. The first to forget is the happiest.

Forgive yourself.

You will become like those you are around the most.

> In some ways friends are like cars — they can take us to new and better places. Cars are great, but being in a car is one of the most physically dangerous things you will ever do. Drive your car carefully. Friends are great, but being with them is one of the most spiritually dangerous things you will ever do. Choose your friends carefully.

People around you will become like you.

> Try to "supersize" the people in your life. Share your faith with your friends, family and coworkers so that as time goes on you will only attend the funerals of Christians.

Thoughts lead to actions, actions lead to habits, habits lead to character and character leads to destiny.

Guard your thoughts.

Thoughts are like rain, and habits are like ruts or gullies that the rain has caused; some good, some bad. Your Mom and I set many of your habits/ruts for you — you're welcome, and we're sorry! It's hard to get out of the bad habits/ruts and easy to fall back into them. The same goes for the good habits.

Nurture good habits.

The best part of fun is anticipation.

The worst part of pain is anticipation.

Don't cry because it's over, smile because it happened.

Expectations

Have low expectations of the world. The world will disappoint you.

Have medium expectations of others. Others will often disappoint you.

Have high expectations of God. God will never disappoint you.

FAITH

I will meditate and be still,

Until something of the overwhelming glory of the truth fall upon me,

and faith begin to realize it:

I am His temple,

and in the secret place He sits upon the throne…

I do now tremblingly accept the blessed truth:

God the Spirit, the Holy Spirit, who is God Almighty

dwells in me.

O my Father

reveal within me what it means,

lest I sin against thee

by saying it and not living it.

Andrew Murray   29

Little faith brings your soul to heaven,
great faith brings heaven to your soul.

Tell God what you'd like for yourself — dream big. "Take delight in the Lord, and he will give you your heart's desires." Psalm 37:4

Tell God what you'd like for others — dream big.

Think about the words when you sing in church; sing like you mean them.

Love God and do what you want. Sounds radical, but anyone who loves Him completely will do what He wants.

We are saints, not sinners. No longer slaves, but free. Don't believe it when Satan tells you that you are no good.

Check your faith progress by looking for more of the fruit of God's Spirit in yourself... love, joy, peace, patience, kindness, goodness, faithfulness, gentleness and self-control.

Remember, God wants spiritual fruit, not religious nuts. In other words, don't be so heavenly minded that you're no earthly good.

Life is like living on a mountain where there is little flat ground; we are either moving up or down. Because of gravity, down is easier. Gravity is like living under the curse — the right way is the hard way. Sometimes we work to climb up, and sometimes we take the easy way and slide down.

We are in a crowd of people, some moving up but most moving down. We are affected by bumping into each other, and sometimes, holding hands or arm in arm, we lead people up or drag them down with us. As we get closer to the narrow peak at the top we get closer to God and to each other. This is especially true in a marriage relationship.

Strive to be a climber, not a slider.

It's normal to have doubts about your faith. Doubt your doubts, and feed your faith. How do you feed your faith? Be in God's Word and pray every day.

Imagine yourself and others as having a light inside of them. This light is the soul. Some people are shining bright; some are very dark. See beyond people's outward appearances and try to brighten their souls.

We become like the people we are around the most, so spend most of your time with "bright light" people. Also, spend a lot of time with God by studying His Word and praying. He is brighter than the noon-day sun.

When bad things happen, don't blame or get mad at God. It's not His fault. Get mad at Satan.

Always be open to God moving you to a mission field.

Ask God for more faith, hope and love. "Three things will last forever — faith, hope, and love — and the greatest of these is love." 1 Corinthians 13:13

Remember, as a Christian, God lives in you.

In the end, when it's all been said and done, it comes down to just you and God.

YOUR BODY

You are fearfully and wonderfully made. "Thank you for making me so wonderfully complex! Your workmanship is marvelous — how well I know it."

Psalm 139:14

Doctors and dentists are our friends. Visit them regularly.

Don't drink much alcohol.

Get out in God's creation as often as you can. It's good for the body and the soul.

Be self-controlled. Let your heart and mind determine your actions, not your body. "I discipline my body like an athlete, training it to do what it should. Otherwise, I fear that after preaching to others I myself might be disqualified."

1 Corinthians 9:27

Appreciate every day that you have good health, but, bodies do wear out — get used to it.

Understand that disease and illness happens.

Understand that pain happens.

Understand that a double chin happens.

Understand that death happens.

Always remember that as a Christian, there's a new body waiting for you that won't get sick, feel pain, get a double chin or die.

Fear knocked, faith answered,
no one was there.

EMOTIONS

Don't trust your feelings too much; feelings change.

Life is about commitments more than feelings.

Don't make a "big thing" out of a little thing.

Learn how to relax your muscles. It will help you feel better. This is why massages feel so good and brighten your mood.

Try not to worry. If you are worrying, maybe it's because you didn't pray; if you prayed, don't worry. A day hemmed with prayer is less likely to unravel.

Worry is like a rocking chair, it gives you something to do but doesn't get you anywhere.

God will give you what you need when you need it.

Face your fears. Don't hide, God will take care of you.

Laughing is one of God's best creations. Make it a habit. "A cheerful heart is good medicine." Proverbs 17:22

Think positive. Negative thinking, anger and bitterness are like acid. They eat away at whatever they are poured on as well as the container they are kept in.

Don't assume too much. If you do, then don't assume the negative about a person or situation; assume the positive.

It's O.K. to cry. Crying is also one of God's best creations.

Remember, nobody's perfect. Cut yourself some slack.

MAJOR ON THE MAJORS

Meaning before money. "Seek the Kingdom of God above all else and live righteously, and he will give you everything you need."

Matthew 6:33

Character before competence. "The LORD doesn't see things the way you see them. People judge by outward appearance, but the LORD looks at the heart."

1 Samuel 16:7

Peace before power. "I am leaving you with a gift—peace of mind and heart. And the peace I give is a gift the world cannot give. So don't be troubled or afraid."   John 14:27

Prayer before pride. "Then if my people who are called by my name will humble themselves and pray and seek my face and turn from their wicked ways, I will hear from heaven and will forgive their sins and restore their land."

2 Chronicles 7:14

Joy before judgement. "Do not judge others, and you will not be judged. Do not condemn others, or it will all come back against you. Forgive others, and you will be forgiven."   Luke 6:37

Service before self. "For even the Son of Man came not to be served but to serve others and to give his life as a ransom for many."   Mark 10:45

Faith before fear. "They do not fear bad news; they confidently trust the LORD to care for them."   Psalm 112:7

Look at yourself. No one is perfect, but do you see... meaning? character? peace? prayer? joy? service? faith? Make it your goal to have more of these qualities in your life. They are available to anyone... all you have to do is ask and believe.

Most of the time we think about the who, what, when, where, and how of life. But, most important is the why.

Every human on earth wants two things... peace and joy. Faith, hope and love are important, but the result of having faith, hope and love is peace and joy. The only true source of joy and peace is God. He created them and created us to desire them.

Ask God to give you more peace and joy. The more you have them the more attractive you and God will be to those around you. Ask God to give your family, friends and enemies more peace and joy. "I pray that God, the source of hope, will fill you completely with joy and peace because you trust in him. Then you will overflow with confident hope through the power of the Holy Spirit."

Romans 15:13

If you don't know how to pray for someone, just pray that God will give them more peace and joy.

RELATIONSHIPS

Don't worry about what others think of you. Care about what God thinks of you.

Remember the 20/20/60 rule. Twenty percent of people you meet will enjoy you. Twenty percent of people you meet won't enjoy you, and sixty percent of the people you meet won't have an opinion either way until they get to know you.

Expect and assume that people will accept and like you. You'll make more friends faster, and make it harder to not enjoy you.

Practice the Matthew 18 principle. "If another believer sins against you, go privately and point out the offense. If the other person listens and confesses it, you have won that person back. But if you are unsuccessful, take one or two others with you and go back again, so that everything you say may be confirmed by two or three witnesses. If the person still refuses to listen, take your case to the church." Matthew 18:15-17

If someone comes to you and wants to complain or put down another person, just say, "Have you talked to that person yet?" Or say, "I'll listen to your complaints only if I'm a part of the problem or a part of the solution."

In other words, don't gossip or listen to gossip.

People are basically the same everywhere, but we have different gifts, strengths and weaknesses.

Look people in the eye.

Listen more than you talk. If we all did that there would be a lot more silence and peace, and we could better hear God's still, small voice. "The heavens proclaim the glory of God. The skies display his craftsmanship. Day after day they continue to speak; night after night they make him known. They speak without a sound or word; their voice is never heard. Yet their message has gone throughout the earth, and their words to all the world." Psalm 19:1-4

It's often hard to do, but when you listen, listen well.

Don't be too hard on your firstborn.

Compare yourself only to Jesus.

Call your parents.

People want better methods,
God wants better people.

LEARNING AND GROWING

Never stop learning.

Be curious.

Ask questions.

Most of life is not black and white but grey.

Don't be afraid to make mistakes. They can be learning opportunities also.

When you stop learning, you start dying.

Most learning comes through experience. Experience is a hard teacher however, as it gives the test first and then the lesson.

If you really want to learn and remember something then teach it to someone else. The teacher learns the most.

Teaching is hard. Appreciate your good teachers.

There are many teachers in the world:

>coworkers
>neighbors
>school teachers
>family
>books and magazines
>TV and movies
>music
>the Bible
>fellow church members
>creation
>God

Don't believe everything you hear. Just because someone is talking from the front of a classroom doesn't mean they have to be your teacher. Think about what they are saying and see if it makes sense in the light of God's Word. Choose your teachers carefully because you will become like them. "Students are not greater than their teacher. But the student who is fully trained will become like the teacher." Luke 6:40

*Wise are those who learn that the bottom line
doesn't always have to be their top priority.*
William Ward

Money and Things

Don't worry about money. "That is why I tell you not to worry about everyday life—whether you have enough food and drink, or enough clothes to wear. Isn't life more than food, and your body more than clothing?" Matthew 6:25

A good rule of thumb is: save 10%, give 10% and spend the rest. "Give, and you will receive. Your gift will return to you in full—pressed down, shaken together to make room for more, running over, and poured into your lap. The amount you give will determine the amount you get back." Luke 6:38

But remember, God doesn't always give back money. Sometimes what He gives is a greater appreciation and joy for what you already have. You can feel rich without being rich.

We can't outgive God. R.G. LeTourneau said, "I shovel it out and God shovels it back, but God has a bigger shovel."

Only go in debt for investments.

Pay your credit card off every month. Credit card debt is like quicksand… easy to get into, but very hard to get out of.

Love people, not things.

Strive to be content, not comfortable.

*The most faithful Follower of God
is the best Leader.*

FUTURE

Expect to be a leader someday. As you learn and mature, your family, friends, coworkers and church will benefit.

We see through a glass darkly.

Plans change.

Goals change.

Circumstances change — be patient.

God never changes.

As we grow, we go through stages in life: unknowing innocence, foolish understanding, establishing worldview, friends and purpose, work and family, wisdom and perspective, reflection and freedom, rest and restoration.

Be open to major life changes at any age:

> Colonel Sanders started his fried chicken franchise when he was in his 60's; Ronald Reagan entered politics at age 54 and became president at age 69; Laura Ingles Wilder published her first book when she was 65; Moses was 80 when he became the leader of the Israelites.

Take a long view of life. When I was 12 and my dad let me steer the car, we swerved back and forth as I struggled to keep it between the lines. He told me to look further down the road, and, to my amazement, the ride became smooth and we also stayed in our lane.

I just recently learned that when there is a curve in the road, if you look as far down the turn as you can the car will track more smoothly through the curve. When life throws you curves, take the long view and enjoy the ride.

A little morbid perhaps, but it can be helpful to think about what your family might write on your tombstone. Will it be like the hypochondriac's tombstone which read, "I told you I was sick!", or something like, "A Godly woman" or "He left the world a better place and went to a better place."

Souls live forever. Look forward with hope. "So be truly glad. There is wonderful joy ahead, even though you have to endure many trials for a little while. These trials will show that your faith is genuine. It is being tested as fire tests and purifies gold—though your faith is far more precious than mere gold."

1 Peter 1:6-7

CONCLUSION

And the last things that I want you to know are:

I'm grateful that you are such great kids!

Thank you for being more patient with me
than I have been with you.

You have blessed my life more than you'll ever know.

I'm proud of you.

I'm praying for you.

I love you.

Dad

ABOUT THE AUTHOR

Chuck and his wife, Cindy, are originally from Minnesota but now reside in Nordegg, Alberta. They are the proud parents of three children, Jared, Katia and Kelly.

Chuck has been a high school teacher, business executive, Christian youth camp director (Frontier Lodge) and most recently started a tour company called Elk Ridge Adventures. Together they operate Miner's Café and Coliseum Gift Shop in Nordegg.

Other interests include reading, inventing, motorcycling and elk hunting.

ACKNOWLEDGEMENTS

I am very grateful for the assistance of a few people in the writing of this book. Sharon took the time to proofread the text and review the photos. Jess made a comprehensive review of every detail and had many great suggestions. Cindy shared her good ideas and was very patient with my frequent questions of "How does this sound?" and "What do you think of this picture?" Without their invaluable help this book would not exist.

PHOTO CREDITS

Most of the photographs in the book were taken by the author or his generous friends. Other photos were supplied by:

Cover art: Ethan Langendoen—fins.cafewall.com

Page 4, 16, 20, 24, 30, 68, 72: Crystalynn Tarr—www.crystalynntarr.com

Page 14: Chris Eason—www.flickr.com/mister-e

Page 42: Greg Peters—www.flickr.com/nc_mountain_man